AUSTIN TRAVEL GUIDE

Where to Go & What to Do

OLIVIA CLARK

No part of this publication may be reproduced, stored in a retrieval system, or transmitted, in any form or by any means without the prior written permission of the publisher, nor be otherwise circulated in any form of binding or cover other than that in which it is published and without similar condition being imposed on the subsequent purchaser. If there are any errors or omissions in copyright acknowledgements the publisher will be pleased to insert the appropriate acknowledgement in any subsequent printing of this publication. Although we have taken all reasonable care in researching this book we make no warranty about the accuracy or completeness of its content and disclaim all liability arising from its use.

Copyright © 2019, Astute Press
All Rights Reserved.

Table of Contents

Austin 7
   Customs & Culture 7
   Geography 8
   Weather & Best Time to Visit 9

Sights & Activities: What to See & Do 10
   Ghost Tours 10
   Haunted Hearse Tours & the Museum of the Weird ... 11
   Austin Steam Train 12
   Austin Zoo 12
   Austin Duck Tours 13
   Dinosaur Park 15
   Texas Capitol Building 16
   Inner Space Cavern 17
   Pioneer Farms 19
   Lady Bird Lake 19
   Lake Travis 20
   Zilker Botanical Garden 20
   Lady Bird Johnson Wildflower Center 21
   Fall Creek Vineyards 22
   Museums 22
        Austin Children's Museum 23
        Texas Natural Science Center 24
        Umlauf Sculpture Garden & Museum 24
        Texas Music Museum 26
        National Museum of the Pacific War 27
        French Legation Museum 28
   State Parks 28
        McKinney Falls State Park 28
        Pedernales Falls State Park 29
        Bastrop State Park 29
        Lockhart State Park 30

Budget Tips 31
   Accommodation 31
        Austin Motel 31
        Adams House Bed and Breakfast 31
        Hostelling International 32
        La Quinta Inn Austin 32
        Americas Best Value Inn 32
   Places to Eat 33
        Ruby's BBQ 33
        Sandy's 33

>> Casino El Camino..33
>> Java Noodles..34
>> El Pollo Regio...34
> Shopping...35
>> Flashback Vintage..35
>> Blue Velvet...35
>> Spring Frost Boutique..35
>> Big Bertha's Bargain Basement..36
>> Ross Dress For Less...36

Know Before You Go..37
> Entry Requirements...37
> Health Insurance..38
> Traveling with Pets..38
> Airports..39
> Airlines...41
> Hubs..43
> Seaports..44
> Money Matters...45
> Currency...45
> Banking-ATMs..45
> Credit Cards...46
> Tourist Tax...46
> Sales Tax..47
> Tipping...47
> Connectivity...48
> Mobile Phones...48
> Dialing Code..49
> Emergency Numbers..49
> General Information...49
> Public Holidays..49
> Time Zones..50
> Daylight Savings Time...51
> School Holidays...51
> Trading Hours..51
> Driving...51
> Drinking...52
> Smoking...53
> Electricity...54
> Food & Drink...54
> American Sports..55
> Useful Websites...57

Austin

Austin, the capital of the state of Texas is the thirteenth largest city in the United States. It was settled in the 1830s and has grown to nearly two million people in the metropolitan area with 800,000 of those people living inside the Austin city limits. Austin is a progressive city full of light, sound, nature and sunshine and is a great choice for a short city break.

Customs & Culture

Austin is known as the Live Music Capital of the World" and musicians can be seen performing in stores, on sidewalks, and in one of the two hundred music venues in the city. Much of the music heard in Austin has roots in the African-American tradition, and include genres such as blues, jazz, and hip-hop.

Many Asian cultures have had a strong influence on the area and the city also prides itself in being an LGBT-friendly and welcoming community. Annual Pride celebrations draws in thousands of outside visitors. Austin celebrates its Celtic heritage annually with food, drink, and traditional Scottish and Irish music.

Texas was a part of Mexico until the middle of the nineteenth century and Mexican culture has played a role in influencing this part of Texas. It is the most notable ethnic culture found in Austin.

Geography

Austin is located in the middle of the state, approximately 350 miles north of South Padre Island at the bottom tip of Texas. Austin is located in the Central Time Zone of North America. The city covers almost 300 square miles and is 489 feet above sea level.

Austin encourages public transportation and ridesharing and offers public transportation on the MetroBus and the MetroRail.

Single Fare: $1.00
Single Fare Reduced: ¢50
Day pass: $2.00

Seniors over 65, people with disabilities, elementary and secondary school students with valid identification, and military members are eligible for reduced fare. If you plan on being in the area for an extended stay, consider buying a week's worth of day passes for $9.00 or a month's worth of day passes for $30, 50% off the price of 30 day passes when bought individually.

Recently, Austin was named as one of the Top 50 Most Walkable Cities so consider walking to your destination but carry water. Walking is also a good way to stay within your budget and get exercise when you're traveling. Biking is another great option. Austin also has coordinated rideshare programs for carpooling.

Weather & Best Time to Visit

Austin's climate is humid and subtropical, meaning the summers are hot. The high temperatures in the summer are usually in the upper 90s and relatively dry. The hottest day on record in Austin, Texas was September 5th, 2000 when the temperature reached 112°F.

The winters are usually very pleasant with average high temperatures in December of 61°F. Only rarely does the temperature dip below freezing and the minimum temperature usually stays above 45°F.

The rainiest season is in the spring, so if you are planning on taking in the sights of Austin in the spring, make sure to bring an umbrella! Sometimes, rain showers turn into thunderstorms, but the actual city very rarely sees any tornado activity. The fall months receive a decent amount of rain, but without the strong thunderstorms. The summer and winter are relatively dry. Winter snow is incredibly rare.

Sights & Activities: What to See & Do

Ghost Tours

Phone: 512.853.9826
Website: www.austinghosttours.com

Walking Tours: $20.00
Trolley Tours: $25.95
Ghost Investigation: $65.00

Austin Ghost Tours has been scaring residents and tourists alike for the past 15 years. The company provide an exciting tour of the city and a paranormal adventure at the same time.

Walking tours go through historical downtown Austin focusing on reputed paranormal and haunted locations.

Trolley tours are available as well. Most tours last for about an hour and a half.

For the serious ghost hunter, a three hours investigation is available with professional ghost-hunters. It may end up being the highlight of your trip.

Tours continue despite the weather, just bring an umbrella. While the walking tour is both stroller and wheelchair accessible, Austin Ghost Tours suggests parents use discretion with children under the age of 10.

SIGHTS & ACTIVITIES: WHAT TO SEE & DO

Austin 360 (Counse, CC BY 2.0)

Haunted Hearse Tours & the Museum of the Weird

Tours begin and end at 701 W 51st Street, Austin, TX
Phone: 512-632-8693

General Admission Rates: $35.00
Tours begin at 8:00 pm and 11:00 pm nightly.

Austin Haunted Hearse Tour take you to fifteen locations in Austin with reputed paranormal activity. During the two hour tour, you are driven through Austin in a Cadillac hearse that has been converted into a limousine. Tours operate with between two and six people.

For an additional $5.00, you can also choose to visit the Austin Museum of the Weird at the end of your tour, saving you $3.00 off of normal admission prices. The museum displays supposed UFO and extraterrestrial activity, Bigfoot sightings and other ghostly encounters.

Austin Steam Train

401 E. Whitestone Blvd., Suite A-103
Cedar Park TX
Phone: 512.477.8468
Email: info@austinsteamtrain.org

The Austin Steam Train offers an interesting perspective into the history of the railroad in Texas and across the United States. This particular railroad was built in the late nineteenth century by the Southern Pacific Railroad Company and was the first railroad in the city.

Ticket prices and hours of operation vary based on the time of the year and the train tour you wish to go on. You can call the Austin Steam Train Association at 512.477.8468. You may also buy tickets and see the train schedule at their website: http://www.austinsteamtrain.org. Any remaining tickets go on sale at the train station an hour and a half before the train leaves.

The Austin Steam Train is a great activity for both children and adults.

Austin Bat Statue (Caomai, CC BY-SA 2.0)

Austin Zoo

10808 Rawhide Trail

Austin, TX
Phone: 512.288.1490

Hours
Summer: 9:30 am-6:00 pm
Winter: 10:00 am-5:30 pm
Closed on Thanksgiving and Christmas Day

General Admission Rates:
Adults: $8.00
Students: $6.00
Seniors: $6.00
Military Personnel (With proper identification): $6.00
Children: $5.00
Member Guests: $5.00

Austin Zoo is rather unique. Rather than breeding animals and bringing in more animals, they are dedicated to taking care of the animals that were abandoned by their owners or rescued from neglectful and abusive situations. Right now, the Austin Zoo is home to over 300 animals, both domestic and exotic. There are many species of monkeys, birds, and reptiles, along with big cats such as panthers. Most of the animals come right up to the fence, so the Austin Zoo provides a unique opportunity to get up close and personal with the animals.

The admission fee and any donations help the zoo continue their mission of helping these animals. Every year, the zoo brings in nearly 200,000 visitors every year.

The zoo is a great place for all ages, and is stroller and wheelchair accessible. The zoo staff recommends wearing closed toe shoes to avoid any walking injuries while touring the zoo. A walking tour of the zoo usually takes around an hour and a half. The staff also welcomes you to bring your own food and beverages to enjoy while touring the zoo or to enjoy in the picnic area.

Austin Duck Tours

209 East 6th Street
Austin, TX 78701
512.477.5274

Tour Start Times:
Monday-Tuesday: 2:00pm
Wednesday-Friday: 11:00 am, 2:00 pm
Saturday-Sunday: 11:00 am, 2:00 pm, 4:00 pm

General Admission Rates:
Adults: $29.95
Seniors: $23.95
Students: $23.95
Children (3-12): $15.95
Children Under 2: Free

The Austin Duck Tours are unlike anything else in the city.

This tour will take you around Lake Austin and the city in an unsinkable Hydra Terra vehicle. Hydra Terra vehicles are unique in the fact that they can drive on land and navigate in the water.

This tour will take you to historical spots across the city, both by land and by water. This is an amazing adventure for both children and adults alike, and will definitely be a highlight of your trip. After all, not many people have the opportunity to ride in a Hydra Terra Vehicle!

The Austin Duck Tours staff encourages you to make reservations in order to ensure your spot on the tour on the day you want. This is especially true if you are traveling around a major holiday or during the summer when tourism to Austin is especially high.

SIGHTS & ACTIVITIES: WHAT TO SEE & DO

Austin City Center (avinashbhat, CC BY-SA 2.0)

Dinosaur Park

893 Union Chapel Road
Cedar Creek, Texas. 78612
Phone: 512.321.6262

General Admission Rate: $7.00
Children under two are free.
Season passes are available for $20.00 per person and are valid for one year after purchase.

Summer Hours
Tuesday-Sunday: 10:00 am-4:00 pm

Winter Hours:
Saturday and Sunday: 10:00 am-:00 pm
Monday-Friday: Reserved for school groups

The Dinosaur Trail at Dinosaur Park is by far the most popular part of the park.

This half-mile trail takes you through a realistic habitat of a dinosaur, complete with life size replicas of dinosaurs that roamed the area hundreds of millions of years ago. You will also see modern day area wildlife while walking through the woods, such as rabbits, lizards, birds, and some pretty cool insects. There are also scavenger hunts and educational opportunities available for children guests. This is definitely a must on your sightseeing list if you have young children.

Texas Capitol Building

112 East 11th Street
Austin, Texas

Hours
Monday-Friday: 7:00 am-10:00 pm
Saturday-Sunday: 9:00 am-8:00 pm

Built in the late nineteenth century, the Texas capitol building is a historically significant building, as well as an amazing piece of architecture. The capitol building and the surrounding acres contain monuments to honor the history behind the city of Austin and the state's government.

While visiting the Capitol building you can decide to show yourself around the capital with the help of some historical information provided by the Visitor's Center. You can also stop into the Visitor's Center to schedule a free tour with one of the building staff.

Austin Natural Spring (karlnorling, CC BY 2.0)

Inner Space Cavern

4200 S. IH-35
Georgetown, Texas
Phone: 512.931.2283
Toll Free: 877.931.2283

Summer Hours:
Monday- Saturday: 9:00 am-6:00 pm
Sunday: 10:00 am-6:00 pm

Winter Hours:
Monday- Friday: 9:00 am-4:00 pm
Saturday: 10:00 am-5:00 pm
Sunday: 11:00 am-5:00 pm
Closed on Thanksgiving, Christmas Eve, and Christmas Day.

While on any tours of the cave, you will have the opportunity to experience the breathtaking beauty that was formed beneath the earth's surface almost one hundred million years ago. The tours only cover a few miles of the total cave. Much of the cave has yet to be explored, and fossils of prehistoric animals are often found throughout the cave.

Adventure Tour

Adults: $19.95

Children (4-12): $11.95
Children (Under 3): Free

The Adventure tour is an hour and fifteen minute tour that is a great place to start if you have never experienced the thrill of walking through caves.

Explorer Tour

Adult: $21.95
Children (4-12): $13.95

This hour and a half long tour is a great choice if you have some experience with exploring caves, but do not want to spend all afternoon in the cave.

Wild Cave Tour

Adults and Children 13+: $100.00
Active members or family of military with proper identification: $80.00

The Wild Cave tour is definitely for those who have had previous experience with caves. It is an extensive four hour tour of the cave.

Children under the age of thirteen are not permitted on this tour. Children who are under the age of 18 must have a parent's signature in order to participate in this tour.

Austin Water View (flamnguitar, CC BY 2.0)

Pioneer Farms

10621 Pioneer Farms Drive
Austin, Texas
Phone: 512.837.1215
Email: farminfo@pioneerfarms.org

Hours:
Friday-Sunday: 10:00 am-5:00 pm

General Admission Rates

Adults: $8.00
Children: $6.00
Children under 2: Free

Pioneer Farm takes you back in time in Texas history and allows you to see how people lived during the 1800s. There are five main attractions to visit while at Pioneer Farms:
1841 Tonkawa Encampment
1868 German Immigrant Farm
1873 Texan Farm
1887 Cotton Planter's Farm
1899 Sprinkle Corner rural village

All of these sites offer an authentic chance to learn and experience the nineteenth century. There is also a barn with contains many friendly animals and many walking trails to explore the entire farm.

Lady Bird Lake

Lady Bird Lake is a manmade lake that was created in 1960. However, just because it is a manmade lake does not mean it lacks for recreational activities! The city of Austin banned the use of motorized water vehicles in Lady Bird Lake, so it is used mostly by canoers and kayakers. Rowing teams also utilize the 470 acre lakes. Swimming in the lake is also not allowed, but sitting on the grass enjoying a picnic by the lake certainly is! Lady Bird Lake is named after Claudia "Lady Bird" Taylor, who was the wife of President Lyndon B. Johnson and the First Lady from 1963-1969.

Lake Travis

Lake Travis is another manmade lake in the area that is fed by the Colorado River. The lake offers over two hundred miles of shoreline perfect for picnicking and camping. Swimming is allowed in this lake, and with a lake that is over two hundred feet deep, many scuba divers as well. Motor boats and fishing is allowed in this lake, and many people enjoy eating the many kinds of bass that swim in the lake, so bring your fishing pole! Fishing poles and canoes are also available for rent.

Downtown Austin (ilovemypit, CC BY 2.0)

Zilker Botanical Garden

2220 Barton Springs Rd
Austin, TX
Phone: 512.477.8672

Hours: 7:00 am-5:30 pm

General Admission Rate:
Children under 3: Free
Children (3-12): $1.00
Adults (13-61): $2.00
Seniors (62+): $1.00

The Zilker Botanical Garden was created in 1955 in an effort encourage education and gardening among people of all ages. Today, the gardens are spread out over 30 acres on the bank of the Colorado River and very near the Lady Bird Lake. Over a quarter of a million visitors from all across the United States come to see the Botanical Garden every year. There are hundreds of different kinds of plants and flowers within the garden, providing a breathtaking sight in comparison to the urban city surrounding the Zilker Botanical Garden.

Lady Bird Johnson Wildflower Center

4801 La Crosse Avenue
Austin, TX
Phone: 512.232.0100

Hours:
Tuesday-Saturday: 9:00 am-5:00 pm
Sunday: 12:00 pm-5:00 pm
Monday: Closed

General Admission Rates:
Adults: $9.00
Seniors (65+): $7.00
Students: $7.00
Children (5-12): $3.00
Children under 5: Free

Named for the wife of President Lyndon B. Johnson, the Lady Bird Johnson Wildflower Center showcases all of the native wildflowers of Texas. With two miles of trails, acres upon acres of gardens, and beautiful bodies of water, this wildflower center is perfect for any nature lover. The Butterfly Garden is unique in that is not an enclosed garden, allowing the butterflies to move freely throughout the Wildflower Center. Butterflies are critically important in a wildflower garden, along with bees, because they pollinate the flowers. Without the help of animals that pollinate, wildflowers would not bloom.

AUSTIN TRAVEL GUIDE

Morning In Austin (StuSeeger, CC BY 2.0)

Fall Creek Vineyards

1820 County Rd. 222
Tow, Texas
Phone: 325.379.5361

Hours
Monday-Friday: 11:00 am-4:00 pm
Saturday: 11:00 am-5:00 pm
Sunday: 12:00 pm-4:00 pm

Despite the 80 mile drive from Austin, Fall Creek Vineyards is an excellent destination for a relaxing afternoon in the sun with your special someone. With many different varieties of wine to sample made from the grapes grown on the vineyard, your tour of the vineyards is sure to be scenic and pleasant.

Museums

The city of Austin is rich in history and learning, demonstrated by the many museums in the city and the surrounding area. Museums are a great way to spend a rainy afternoon or a quiet day without a lot of running around. These following museums are some of the best museums in the area.

Austin Children's Museum

201 Colorado Street
Austin, Texas 78701
Phone: 512-472-2499

Hours:
Tuesday- Saturday: 10:00 am-5:00 pm
Sunday: 12:00 pm-5:00 pm

General Admission Rates:
Adult: $6.50
Children (2+ years): $6.50
Children (12- 23 months): $4.50
Children (Under 12 months): Free

The Austin Children's Museum is a great destination if it suddenly rains and you need to entertain your children for the afternoon. This museum has many educational exhibits for children of all ages. The current featured exhibit teaches children about gravity, inertia, and momentum. Permanent exhibits include the Global City, the Funstruction Zone, which features large building blocks to construct whatever the heart desires, and the Rising Star Ranch. The Rising Star Ranch is for children under the age of two and features many different interactive games for you to enjoy with your toddler!

Outdoor Band (flamnguitar, CC BY 2.0)

Texas Natural Science Center

2400 Trinity Street
Austin, TX
Phone: 512.471.1604

Hours:
Monday- Thursday: 9:00 am-5:00 pm
Friday: 9:00 am-4:45 pm
Saturday: 10:00 am-4:45 pm
Sunday: 1:00 pm-4:45

The Museum is closed Thanksgiving, Christmas Eve and Christmas Day, New Year's Eve and New Year's Day, Easter, and Independence Day.

Admission: Free!

The Texas Natural Science Center is definitely a place to stop while you are visiting. This museum is educational, fun, and best of all, completely affordable. The center has four indoor exhibits and additional outdoor exhibits. This science center is home to thousands of different fossils. The Hall of Geology and Paleontology takes you back hundreds of millions of years ago when dinosaurs and other animals roamed the earth, a long before the modern human came around. The hall contains over five hundred fossils of dinosaurs, other animals, and plants.

The Great Hall shows off the most valuable and rare fossils that the museum owns. One such fossil, the Texas Pterosaur had a wingspan of almost forty feet, much longer than the wingspan of the winged creatures we see flying around today. The Hall of Texas Wildlife showcases fossils of animals that have been found in the area in more recent future, including mammals, birds, and reptiles. The Hall of Biodiversity is a little bit different than the other indoor exhibits. Instead of focusing only on fossils, this hall offers some different educational opportunities about science in general.

Umlauf Sculpture Garden & Museum

605 Robert E. Lee Road
Austin, TX
Phone: 512.445.5582

Hours:
Monday-Tuesday: Closed
Wednesday-Friday: 10:00am-4:30pm
Saturday-Sunday: 1:00pm-4:30pm

General Admission
Adults: $3.50
Students: $1.50
Seniors: $2.50
Children under 6: Free

The sculptures that are featured in this museum are the works of Charles Umlauf. Umlauf was a world famous sculptor in the twentieth century who was an art professor at the University of Texas, Austin. The museum and the garden is run by volunteers who appreciate the life and work of Charles Umlauf and want to share his sculptures with others. The admission charge is definitely affordable, and this museum is perfect for the art lover.

Texas State Capitol (Aleksandr Zykov, CC BY-SA 2.0)

Texas Music Museum

1009 East 11th Street
Austin, TX
Phone: 512.472.8891

Hours:
Monday-Friday: 9:00 am-4:30 pm
Saturday-Sunday: Closed

General Admission Rates:
Free for most exhibits and special events

The Texas Music Museum celebrates the diverse and colorful past and present of music in Texas. Admission to this museum is free, but free will donations are accepted and appreciated to keep the dream of this museum's founders alive. Tours are usually self-guided, but school and private tours by one of the knowledgeable volunteer staff are also offered by contacting the museum at 512.472.8891. This is a perfect destination for the music lover who is in Austin to appreciate the "Live Music Capital of the World"

National Museum of the Pacific War

340 East Main Street
Fredericksburg, TX
Phone: 830.997.8600

Hours:
Monday-Sunday: 9:00 am-5:00 pm

General Admission Rates
Adults: $14.00
Seniors (62+): $12.00
WWII Veterans: Free

Military personnel (with proper identification):

Students: $7.00
Children: $7.00
Children under 6: Free

This museum is entirely dedicated to those who fought in the military in the Pacific Ocean during World War II. Fleet Admiral Nimitz, the commander of over two million men and women in the Pacific Ocean, was born in Fredericksburg, Texas, so this town was given the honor of hosting this museum. The funds to build a Japanese Peace Garden were provided by the Japanese government in the years after WWII as a symbol of friendship and peace between the two countries. As a way of thanking the men and women who served in WWII, the museum offers free admission to WWII veterans.

Texas State Capitol Building (Aleksandr Zykov, CC BY-SA 2.0)

French Legation Museum

802 San Marcos Street
Austin, TX
Phone: 512.472.8180

Hours:
Tuesday-Sunday: 1:00 pm-5:00 pm
Monday: Closed

General Admission Rates: $5.00

The French Legation Museum is run by the Daughters of the Republic of Texas and was built in 1956 as a way to promote the history and culture of Texas. This museum consists of a small house and kitchen that are replicas of houses that women would have kept in nineteenth century Texas. There is also a park that is free and open for use by the public. Pets are welcome, as are picnickers, so grab a lunch and enjoy the afternoon after your tour.

State Parks

McKinney Falls State Park

5808 McKinney Falls Parkway
Austin, TX
Phone: 512.243.1643

Open year round from 8:00 am- 10:00 pm.

General Admission Rates:
Adults: $6.00
Children under 12: Free

McKinney Falls State Park is a perfect destination when you just need a day off from constantly running around. Visitors to McKinney enjoy fishing, the small, but nevertheless majestic waterfall, and wading in the small resulting lake. There are also options for biking, picnicking, and camping.

Pedernales Falls State Park

2585 Park Road 6026
Johnson City, TX
Phone: 830.868.7304

Hours: Open year round

Adult General Admission: $5.00
Children under 12: Free

The Pedernales Falls State Park is not directly in Austin, but the scenery is worth the drive. Camping and picnicking are popular activities, as well as hiking, biking, and horseback riding. There are many different species of birds living in the park as well, so pick up a checklist of different birds at the park's Main Office.

Swimming and tubing are also popular in the Pedernales River, and when the average high temperature in July is 92°F, the water is certainly refreshing. However, the Pedernales River is infamous for flash floods, so be prepared to leave the river immediately and head to higher ground if the water starts to rise. It's a good idea to check weather alerts frequently when spending time in and around the water.

Bastrop State Park

3005 Highway 21 East
Bastrop, TX
Phone: 512.321.2101

Open year round

Adult General Admission: $4
Children under 12: Free

Bastrop State Park is about a 40 mile drive from Austin, but is another park that is worth it! This State Park contains part of the "Lost Pines", which are thought to be the remnants of a massive prehistoric pine forest. The trees that are in the State Park are protected from further destruction of logging or fire.

Bastrop State Park is also home to the Lost Pines Golf Course, which is the most scenic golf course in the area. The beautiful weather in central Texas ensures the golf course can be utilized year round. Golf carts and pull carts are available for rent. There is also a miniature golf course available for the younger golfers.

As with many State Parks, camping and picnicking are popular activities. The park also rents out canoes, and many enjoy fishing or simply being on the water.

Lockhart State Park

4179 State Park Road
Lockhart, TX 78644-9716
Phone: 512.398.3479

Hours: Open year round

General Admission Rates: $3.00
Kids under 12: Free

Lockhart State Park is located about 40 miles south of Austin. This beautiful state park offers camping, fishing, and picnicking, as well as hiking and a golf course. The golf course is the only state park golf course that is operated by State Park employees. Golf clubs and carts are available for rent at the main office. Lockhart State Park also offers education programs for children and adults. Activities include stargazing and night hikes, bird watching, and conservation programs.

Budget Tips

Accommodation

Austin Motel

1220 South Congress Avenue
Austin, TX
Phone: 512.441.1157
Email: reservations@austinmotel.com

The Austin Motel is a funky little motel in a trendy neighborhood.

Bedrooms that sleep up to two people run for about $110.00 per night, which is much more affordable than some of the higher end hotels in the area. The Austin Motel is on South Congress Avenue, sometimes known as SoCo, which has some of the best places for shopping and food. There are also bars and nightclubs in the area.

Adams House Bed and Breakfast

4300 Avenue G
Austin, TX
512.453.7696
Email: reservations@theadamshouse.com

Considered to be a historic landmark, the Adams House Bed and Breakfast is a popular place to stay. Rooms start at $129.00 per night for two people. Rooms include free Wi-Fi connection, air conditioning and central heat, a hairdryer, and bottled water. There is also an iron and ironing board in the common area, as well as couches to relax on while watching television or a movie. The Adams House also offers a free and organic breakfast from 7:00 am- 9:00 am during the week and starting at 9:00 am on the weekends.

While the Adams House is not in downtown, there are many different things to do in the area. There are many popular restaurants within walking distance, as well as many sightseeing opportunities. This out of the way bed and breakfast is the perfect way to stay while in Austin.

Hostelling International

2200 South Lakeshore Blvd
Austin, TX
Phone: 512.444.2294

If you are really looking for a bargain while staying in the area, a hostel makes a great place to stay. A bed for one night runs a person about $22.00, so this is a great choice if you are traveling alone and have no need for a room for yourself. It's also a great way to budget in general. Sheets are included at this hostel, so no need to bring your own. Hostels provide a great opportunity to meet other travelers to the area.

Hostelling International Austin also is very environmentally friendly, and often hosts events with the city to pick up trash and volunteer in public parks and gardens to keep the city of Austin looking beautiful.

La Quinta Inn Austin

300 East 11th St
Austin, TX 78701
Phone: 512.476.1166

The La Quinta Inn is a very inclusive stay for only $115.00 per night for one room. This Inn boasts an outdoor pool, business center, free Wi-FI connection, fitness center, and is also pet friendly. La Quinta also offers a delicious free breakfast, which includes cereals, waffles, fresh fruit, and all the coffee and juice you can drink.

Americas Best Value Inn

909 E. Koenig Lane
Austin, TX
512.452.4200

Americas Best Value Inn really lives up to its name. Before any discounts, one room is about $62.00 per night. Discounts are available for seniors, military members, and government employees. This inn offers Wi-Fi connection, an outdoor pool, business and meeting areas, an exercise center, laundry services and a continental breakfast.

Places to Eat

Ruby's BBQ

512 West 29th Street,
Austin, TX
Phone: 512.477.1651
Email: info@rubysbbq.com

Founded in 1988, the initial goal of Ruby's BBQ was to offer quality, affordable food for the University of Texas students and the surrounding area. This BBQ restaurant does not only offer quality meat, but soups, salads, and vegetarians options as well. However, most people who visit Ruby's enjoy their brisket, chicken, or ribs.

The meat is cooked in the brick pits that are no longer used in many restaurants. Brick pits require wood as well as a lot of human involvement in the cooking process which many larger restaurants cannot use due to the restricted amount of meat they can cook at one time. Ruby's also makes all of its side dishes on site, so you know your meal is fresh! Entree prices range from $5.00 to $15.00, making Ruby's an unbeatable restaurant.

Sandy's

603 Barton Springs Road
Austin, TX
Phone: 512.478.6322

Hours:
Monday-Sunday: 10:30 am-10:30 pm

Some would say that Sandy's is one of the best kept secrets when it comes to hamburgers. Sandy's is an old fashioned hamburger joint that offers hamburgers, French fries, hot dogs, root beer floats, and custard. The hamburgers are no-nonsense and come with the basic trimmings of a good hamburger. It is not hard to get a great hamburger basket and a drink for less than $5.00.

Casino El Camino

517 East 6th Street

Austin, TX 78701
Phone: 512.469.9330

When you have a late night craving for an amazing burger, Casino El Camino is the place for you as the kitchen in this bar stays open until 1:30 am. Casino El Camino offers burgers, chicken wings, hot dogs, and assorted cold sandwiches. The food has been named the best bar food in Austin and has been featured on the Food Network show "Diners, Drive-ins, and Dives". Even better, no entree on the menu is more than $9.00, and the meat they use in their dishes is from environmentally sustainable, small, local farms.

Java Noodles

2400 East Oltorf Street #14
Austin, TX
Phone: 512.443.5282

Java Noodles is an awesome place to stop when you are craving Indonesian inspired food. The entrees are under $10.00, which is helpful when traveling on a budget. The restaurant also accommodates those who follow vegetarian or vegan diets, as well as offering many entrees for picky children.

El Pollo Regio

6615 Berkman Drive
Austin, TX
Phone: 512.933.9557

Brought to Austin from Mexico in 1995, this marinated chicken has been popular with Texans for years. While the first location was opened in Austin, this restaurant has many different locations in Texas. The prices are surprising considering the amount and quality of food you receive. An order of 16 pieces of chicken, along with two orders of rice, two orders of beans, two orders of tortillas, and salsa only costs a little over $20.00. If you don't need a family size order of food, two pieces of chicken with sides of rice, beans, and tortillas will only set you back about $4.00.

Shopping

Flashback Vintage

1805 S 1st Street
Austin, TX
Phone: 512.445.6906

Flashback has been an amazing place to shop since 1982. Flashback is far from your neighborhood thrift store, offering high end and designer vintage clothing.

Flashback accepts vintage pieces in good condition to resell to the public. Shopping 'vintage' is popular among many groups of people today, helps save money, and is quite environmentally friendly. Flashback carries men's and women's clothing that will help you create a look that is all your own. Employees are knowledgeable, helpful, and friendly, and will help you achieve your desired look.

Blue Velvet

217 W. North Loop Blvd
Austin, TX
Phone: 512.452.2583
Email: bvvintage@gmail.com

Monday-Sunday: 11 am-8 pm

Another famous vintage store in the area, Blue Velvet will help you find an outfit for whatever occasion you are shopping for. Blue Velvet makes a point to buy clothing in all different sizes in an effort to cater to all body types. Blue Velvet has men's clothing and shoes, women's clothing and shoes, as well as accessories.

Spring Frost Boutique

5101 Burnet Road
Austin, TX
Phone: 512.467.9100

Hours:

Monday-Saturday: 10:00 am-6:00 pm

Spring Frost Boutique is a great place to shop if you are looking for designer clothing but are not willing to pay designer prices. This boutique offers designer clothing for up to 75% off the designer's asking price, so while the prices may be a little higher than at other stores, the quality of clothing you find there is unbeatable. The staff is knowledgeable and friendly, and will help to whatever extent they are needed. If you are not a fan of shopping, the staff will do the finding for you and bring you different pieces to try on while you relax with a glass of wine in the fitting room. They will also go out of their way to make sure your shopping trip is enjoyable and comfortable.

Big Bertha's Bargain Basement

1050 South Lamar Boulevard
Austin, TX
Phone: 512.444.5908

Big Bertha's Bargain Basement is a great place to shop if you are looking for last season's pieces. You will not pay full price for anything in this store, regardless of whether it is new or used.

Ross Dress For Less

5400 Brodie Ln # 500
Austin, TX
Phone: 512-892-2874

While Ross Dress for Less is a chain store, you will have a unique shopping experience at each store, and the Austin location is no different. Ross carries clothing, accessories, and shoes for men, women, and children. Many of the brands are designer but are sold for half of what they sell for in department stores. Ross also prides itself in being a socially responsible company, treating all of its employees ethically and providing products that have been made in an environmentally sustainable way

Know Before You Go

Entry Requirements

The Visa Waiver Programme (VWP) allows nationals of selected countries to enter the United States for tourism or certain types of business without requiring a visa. This applies to citizens of the UK, Australia, New Zealand, Canada, Chile, Denmark, Belgium, Austria, Latvia, Estonia, Finland, Italy, Hungary, Iceland, France, Germany, Japan, Spain, Portugal, Norway, Sweden, Slovenia, Slovakia, Switzerland, Brunei, Taiwan, South Korea, Luxemburg, Singapore, Liechtenstein, Monaco, Malta, San Marino, Lithuania, Greece, the Netherlands and the Czech Republic. To qualify, you will also need to have a passport with integrated chip, also known as an e-Passport. The e-Passport symbol has to be clearly displayed on the cover of the passport. This secure method of identification will protect and verify the holder in case of identity theft and other breaches of privacy. There are exceptions. Visitors with a criminal record, serious communicable illness or those who were deported or refused entry on a past occasion will not qualify for the Visa Waiver Program and will need to apply for a visa. Holders of a UK passport who have dual citizenship of Iraq, Iran, Sudan, Syria, Somalia, Libya or Yemen (or those who have travelled to the above countries after 2011) will also need to apply for a visa. A requirement of the Visa Waiver Programme is online registration with the Electronic System for Travel Authorisation (ESTA) at least 72 hours before your travels. When entering the United States, you will be able to skip the custom declaration and proceed directly to an Automated Passport Control (APC) kiosk.

If travelling from a non-qualifying country, you will need a visitor's visa, also known as a non-immigrant visa when entering the United States for visiting friends or family, tourism or medical procedures. It is recommended that you schedule your visa interview at least 60 days before your date of travel. You will need to submit a passport that will be valid for at least 6 months after your intended travel, a birth certificate, a police certificate and color photographs that comply with US visa requirements. Proof of financial support for your stay in the United States is also required.

Health Insurance

Medical procedures are very expensive in the United States and there is no free or subsidized healthcare service. The best strategy would be to organize temporary health insurance for the duration of your stay. You will not need any special vaccinations if visiting the United States as tourists. For an immigration visa, the required immunizations are against hepatitis A and B, measles, mumps, rubella, influenza, polio, tetanus, varicella, meningococcal, pneumococcal, rotavirus, pertussis and influenza type B.

There are several companies that offer short-term health insurance packages for visitors to the United States. Coverage with Inbound USA can be purchased online through their website and offer health insurance for periods from 5 to 364 days. Visitor Secure will provide coverage for accidents and new health complications from 5 days to 2 years, but the cost and care of pre-existing medical conditions and dental care is excluded. Inbound Guest offers similar terms for periods of between 5 and 180 days and will email you a virtual membership card as soon as the contract is finalized. Physical cards will be available within one business day of arrival to the United States.

Traveling with Pets

The United States accepts EU pet passports as valid documentation for pets in transit, provided that your pet is up to date on vaccinations. In most instances, the airline you use will require a health certificate. While microchipping is not required, it may be helpful in case your pet gets lost. If visiting from a non-English speaking country, be sure to have an English translation of your vet's certificate available for the US authorities to examine. To be cleared for travel, your pet must have a vet's certificate issued no less than 10 days before your date of travel. Pets need to be vaccinated against rabies at least 30 days prior to entry to the United States. If the animal was recently microchipped, the microchipping procedure should have taken place prior to vaccination. In the case of dogs, it is also important that your pet must test negative for screwworm no later than 5 days before your intended arrival in the United States.

In the case of exotic pets such as parrots, turtles and other reptiles, you will need check on the CITES (Convention on International Trade in

Endangered Species of Wild Fauna and Flora) status of the breed, to ensure that you will in fact be allowed to enter the United States with your pet. There are restrictions on bringing birds from certain countries and a quarantine period of 30 days also applies for birds, such as parrots. It is recommended that birds should enter the United States at New York, Los Angeles or Miami, where quarantine facilities are available. The owner of the bird will carry the expense of the quarantine and advance reservations need to be made for this, to prevent the bird being refused entry altogether. Additionally, you will need to submit documentation in the form of a USDA import permit as well as a health certificate issued by your veterinarian less than 30 days prior to the date of entry.

Airports

Your trip will probably be via one of the country's major gateway airports. **Hartsfield–Jackson Atlanta International Airport** (ATL), which is located less than 12km from the central business area of Atlanta in Georgia is the busiest airport in the United States and the world. It processes about 100 million passengers annually. Internationally, it offers connections to Paris, London, Frankfurt Amsterdam, Dubai, Tokyo, Mexico City and Johannesburg. Domestically, its busiest routes are to Florida, New York, Los Angeles, Dallas and Chicago. Delta Airlines maintains a huge presence at the airport, with the largest hub to be found anywhere in the world and a schedule of almost a thousand daily flights. Via a railway station, the airport provides easy access to the city.

Los Angeles International Airport (LAX) is the second busiest airport in the United States and the largest airport in the state of California. Located in the southwestern part of Los Angeles about 24km from the city center, it is easily accessibly by road and rail. Its nine passenger terminals are connected through a shuttle service. Los Angeles International Airport is a significant origin-and-destination airport for travellers to and from the United States. The second busiest airport in California is **San Francisco International Airport** (SFO) and, like Los Angeles it is an important gateway for trans-Pacific connections. It serves as an important maintenance hub for United and is home to an aviation museum. Anyone who is serious about green policies and environmentally friendly alternatives will love San Francisco's airport. There is a special bicycle route to the airport, designated bicycle parking zones and even a service that offers special freight units for travelling with your bicycle. Bicycles are also allowed on its Airtrain service. The third airport of note in California is **San Diego International Airport** (SAN).

Chicago O'Hare International Airport (ORD) is located about 27km northwest of Chicago's central business district, also known as the Chicago Loop. As a gateway to Chicago and the Great Lakes region, it is the US airport that sees the highest frequency of arrivals and departures. Terminal 5 is used for all international arrivals and most international departures, with the exception of Air Canada and some airline carriers under the Star Alliance or Oneworld brand. The Airport Transit System provides easy access for passengers between terminals and to the remote sections of the parking area.

Located roughly halfway between the cities of Dallas and Fort Worth, **Dallas-Fort Worth International Airport** (DFW) is the primary international airport serving the state of Texas. Both in terms of passenger numbers and air traffic statistics, it ranks among the ten busiest airports in the world. It is also home to the second largest hub in the world, that of American Airlines, which is headquartered in Texas. Through 8 Interstate highways and 3 major rail services, it provides access to the city centers of both Dallas and Fort Worth, as well as the rest of Texas. An automated people mover, known as the Skylink makes it effortless for passenger to transverse between different sections of the airport and the parking areas. Terminal D is its international terminal. The second busiest airport in Texas is the **George Bush Intercontinental Airport** (IAH) in Houston, which offers connections to destinations across the United States, as well as Mexico, Canada, the Americas and selected cities in Europe and Asia.

John F. Kennedy International Airport (JFK) is located in the neighborhood of Queens. In terms of international passengers, it is one of the busiest airports in the United States, with connections to 6 continents and with the air traffic of 70 different airlines. Its busiest routes are to London, Paris, Los Angeles and San Francisco. It serves as a gateway hub for both Delta and American Airlines. Terminal 8, its newest terminal, is larger than Central Park. It has the capacity of processing around 1600 passengers per hour. An elevated railway service, the Airtrain provides access to all 8 of its terminals and also connects to the Long Island railroad as well as the New York City Subway in Queens. Within the airport, the service is free. Three other major airports also service the New

York City area. **Newark Liberty International Airport** (EWR) is New York's second busiest airport and home of the world's third largest hub, that of United Airlines. Newark is located about 24km from Mid Manhattan, between Newark and Elizabeth. Its airtrain offers an easy way of commuting around the airport and connects via the Newark Liberty International Airport Station to the North Jersey Coast line and Northeast Corridor line. Other airports in New York are **La Guardia Airport** (LGA), located on the Flushing Bay Waterfront in Queens and **Teterboro Airport** (TEB), which is mainly used by private charter companies.

Washington D.C. is served by two airports, **Baltimore-Washington International Airport** (BWI) and **Washington Dulles International Airport** (IAD). Other important airports on the eastern side of the United States include **Logan International Airport** (BOS) in Boston, **Philadelphia International Airport** (PHL) and **Charlotte Douglas International Airport** (CLT) in North Carolina. The three busiest airports in the state of Florida are **Miami International Airport** (MIA), **Fort Lauderdale-Hollywood International Airport** (FLL) and **Tampa International Airport** (TPA). In the western part of the United States, **McCarran International Airport** (LAS) in Las Vegas and **Phoenix Sky Harbor International** (PHX) in Arizona offer important connections. **Denver International Airport** (DEN) in Colorado is the primary entry point to Rocky Mountains, while **Seattle-Tacoma International Airport** (SEA) in Washington State and **Portland International Airport** (PDX) in Oregon provide access to the Pacific Northwest. **Honolulu International Airport** (HNL) is the primary point of entry to Hawaii.

Airlines

The largest air carriers in the United States are United Airlines, American Airlines and Delta Airlines. Each of these could lay claim to the title of largest airline using different criteria. In terms of passenger numbers, Delta Airlines is the largest airline carrier. It was founded from humble beginnings as a crop dusting outfit in the 1920s, but grew to an enormous operation through mergers with Northeast Airlines in the 1970s, Western Airlines in the 1980s and North-western Airlines in 2010. Delta also absorbed a portion of Pan Am's assets and business, following its bankruptcy in the early 1990s. Delta Airlines operates Delta Connections, a regional service covering North American destinations in Canada,

Mexico and the United States. In terms of destinations, United Airlines is the largest airline in the United States and the world. Its origins lie in an early airline created by Boeing in the 1920s, but the company grew from a series of acquisitions and mergers - most recently with Continental Airlines - to its current status as a leading airline. Regional services are operated under the brand United Express, in partnership with a range of feeder carriers including CapeAir, CommutAir, ExpressJet, GoJet Airlines, Mesa Airlines, Republic Airlines, Shuttle America, SkyWest Airlines and Trans State Airlines. American Airlines commands the largest fleet in the United States. It originated from the merger of over 80 tiny regional airlines in the 1930s and has subsequently merged with Trans Caribbean Airways, Air California, Reno Air, Trans World Airlines and, most recently, US Airways. Through the Oneworld Airline Alliance, American Airlines is partnered with British Airways, Finnair, Iberia and Japan Airlines. Regional connections are operated under the American Eagle brand name and include the services of Envoy Air, Piedmont Airlines, Air Wisconsin, SkyWest Airlines, Republic Airlines and PSA Airlines. American Airlines operates the American Airlines Shuttle, a service that connects the cities of New York, Boston and Washington DC with hourly flights on weekdays.

Based in Dallas, Texas, Southwest Airlines is the world's largest budget airline. It carries the highest number of domestic passengers in the United States and operates over 200 daily flights on its 3 busiest routes, namely Chicago, Washington and Las Vegas. JetBlue Airways is a budget airline based in Long Island that operates mainly in the Americas and the Caribbean. It covers 97 destinations in the United States, Mexico, Costa Rica, Puerto Rico, Grenada, Peru, Colombia, Bermuda, Jamaica, the Bahamas, Barbados, the Dominican Republic and Trinidad and Tobago. Spirit Airlines is an ultra low cost carrier which offers flights to destinations in the United States, Latin America, Mexico and the Caribbean. It is based in Miramar, Florida.

Alaska Airlines was founded in the 1930s to offer connections in the Pacific Northwest, but began to expand from the 1990s to include destinations east of the Rocky Mountains as well as connections to the extreme eastern part of Russia. Alaska Airlines recently acquired the brand, Virgin America which represents the Virgin brand in the United States. Silver Airways is a regional service which offers connections to various destinations in Florida, Pennsylvania, Virginia and West Virginia and provides a service to several islands within the Bahamas. Frontier Airlines is a relatively new budget airline that is mainly focussed on connections around the Rocky Mountain states. Hawaiian Airlines is based in Honolulu and offers connections to the American mainland as well as to Asia. Island Air also serves Hawaii and enjoys a partnership with United Airlines. Mokulele Airlines is a small airline based in Kona Island. It provides access to some of the smaller airports in the Hawaiian Islands. Sun Country Airlines is based in Minneapolis and covers destinations in the United States, Mexico, Costa Rica, Puerto Rica, Jamaica, St Maarten and the US Virgin Islands. Great Lakes Airline is a major participant in the Essential Air Service, a government programme set up to ensure that small and remote communities can be reached by air, following the deregulation of certified airlines. These regional connections include destinations in Arizona, Colorado, Kansas, Minnesota, Nebraska, New Mexico, South Dakota and Wyoming. In the past, Great Lakes Airline had covered a wide range of destinations as a partner under the United Express banner.

Hubs

Hartsfield Jackson Atlanta International Airport serves as the largest hub and headquarters of Delta Airlines. John F. Kennedy International Airport serves as a major hub for Delta's traffic to and from the European continent. Los Angeles International Airport serves as a hub for Delta Airline's connections to Mexico, Hawaii and Japan, but also serves the Florida-California route. Detroit Metropolitan Wayne County Airport is Delta's second largest hubs and serves as a gateway for connections to Asia.

Washington Dulles International Airport serves as a hub for United Airlines as well as Silver Airways. United Airlines also use Denver International Airport, George Bush Intercontinental Airport in Houston, Los Angeles International Airport, San Francisco International Airport, Newark Liberty International Airport and O'Hare International Airport in Chicago as hubs.

Dallas/Fort Worth International Airport serves as the primary hub for American Airlines. Its second largest hub in the south-eastern part of the US is Charlotte Douglas International Airport in North Carolina and its largest hub in the north is O'Hare International Airport in Chicago. Other hubs for American Airlines are Phoenix Sky Harbor International Airport - its largest hub in the west - Miami International Airport, Ronald Reagan Washington National Airport, Los Angeles International Airport, John F Kennedy International Airport in New York, which serves as a key hub for European air traffic and La Guardia Airport also in New York.

Seattle-Tacoma International Airport serves as a primary hub for Alaska Airlines. Other hubs for Alaska include Portland International Airport, Los Angeles International Airport and Ted Stevens - Anchorage International Airport. Virgin America operates a primary hub at San Francisco International Airport, but also has a second hub at Los Angeles International Airport as well as a significant presence at Dallas Love Field. Denver International Airport is the primary hub for Frontier Airlines, which also has hubs at Chicago O'Hare International Airport and Orlando International Airport. Frontier also maintains a strong presence at Hartsfield-Jackson Atlanta International Airport, Cincinnati/North Kentucky International Airport, Cleveland Hopkins International Airport, McCarran International Airport in Las Vegas and Philadelphia International Airport. Honolulu International Airport and Kahului Airport serve as hubs for Hawaiian Airlines. Mokulele Airlines uses Kona International Airport and Kahului Airport as hubs. Minneapolis–Saint Paul International Airport serves as a hub for Delta Airlines, Great Lakes Airlines and Sun Country Airlines. Silver Airways uses Fort Lauderdale-Hollywood International Airport as a primary hub and also has hubs at Tampa International Airport, Orlando International Airport and Washington Dulles International Airport.

Seaports

The Port of Miami is often described as the cruise capital of the world, but it also serves as a cargo gateway to the United States. There are 8 passenger terminals and the Port Miami Tunnel, an undersea tunnel connects the port to the Interstate 95 via the Dolphin Expressway. Miami is an important base for several of the world's most prominent cruise lines, including Norwegian Cruise Lines, Celebrity Cruises, Royal Caribbean International and Carnival Cruises. In total, over 40 cruise ships representing 18 different cruise brands are berthed at Miami. Well over 4 million passengers are processed here annually. There are two other important ports in the state of Florida. Port Everglades is the third busiest cruise terminal in Florida, as well as its busiest cargo terminal. It is home to *Allure of the Seas* and *Oasis of the Seas*, two of the world's largest cruise ships. Oceanfront condominium dwellers often bid ships farewell with a friendly cacophony of horns and bells. The third important cruise port in Florida is Port Canaveral, which has 5 cruise terminals.

With its location on the Mississippi river, New Orleans is an important cargo port, but it also has a modern cruise terminal with over 50 check-in counters. The Port of Seattle is operated by the same organization that runs the city's airport. It has two busy cruise terminals. The Port of Los Angeles has a state of the art World Cruise Center, with three berths for passenger liners. As the oldest port on the Gulf of Mexico, the Port of Galveston dates back to the days when Texas was still part of Mexico. Galveston serves both as a cargo port and cruise terminal.

Money Matters

Currency

The currency of the United States is US dollar (USD). Notes are issued in denominations of $1, $2, $5, $10, $20, $50 and $100. Coins are issued in denominations of $1 (known as a silver dollar, 50c (known as a half dollar), 25c (quarter), 10c (dime), 5c (nickel) and 1c (penny).

Banking-ATMs

ATM machines are widely distributed across the United States and are compatible with major networks such as Cirrus and Plus for international bank transactions. Most debit cards will display a Visa or MasterCard affiliation, which means that you may be able to use them as a credit card as well. A transaction fee will be charged for withdrawals, but customers of certain bank groups such as Deutsche Bank and Barclays, can be charged smaller transaction fees or none at all, when using the ATM machines of Bank of America. While banking hours will vary, depending on the location and banking group, you can generally expect most banks to be open between 8.30am and 5pm. You will be asked for ID in the form of a passport, when using your debit card for over-the-counter transactions.

While you cannot open a bank account in the United States without a social security number, you may want to consider obtaining a pre-paid debit card, where a fixed amount can be pre-loaded. This service is available from various credit card companies in the United States. The American Express card is called Serve and can be used with a mobile app. You can load more cash at outlets of Walmart, CVS Pharmacy, Dollar General, Family Dollar, Rite Aid and participating 7/Eleven stores.

Credit Cards

Credit cards are widely used in the United States and the the major cards - MasterCard, Visa, American Express and Diners Club – are commonly accepted. A credit card is essential in paying for hotel accommodation or car rental. As a visitor, you may want to check about the fees levied on your card for foreign exchange transactions. While Europe and the UK have already converted to chip-and-pin credit card, the transition is still in progress in the United States. Efforts are being made to make the credit cards of most US stores compliant with chip-and-pin technology. You may find that many stores still employ the older protocols at point-of-sales. Be sure to inform your bank or credit card vendor of your travel plans before leaving home.

Tourist Tax

In the United States, tourist tax varies from city to city, and can be charged not only on accommodation, but also restaurant bills, car rental and other services that cater mainly to tourists. In 22 states, some form of state wide tax is charged for accommodation and 38 states levy a tax on car rental. The city that levies the highest tax bill is Chicago. Apart from a flat fee of $2.75, you can expect to be charged 16 percent per day on hotel accommodation as well as nearly 25% for car rentals. New York charges an 18 percent hotel tax, as does Nashville, while Kansas City, Houston and Indianapolis levy around 17 percent per day hotel tax. Expect to pay 16.5 percent tax per day on your hotel bill in Cleveland and 15.6 percent per day in Seattle, with a 2 percent hike, if staying in the Seattle Tourism Improvement Area. Las Vegas charges 12 percent hotel tax. In Los Angeles, you will be charged a whopping 14 percent on your hotel room, but in Burbank, California, the rate is only 2 percent. Dallas, Texas only charges 2 percent on hotels with more than a hundred rooms. In Portland a city tax of 6 percent is added to a county tax of 5.5 percent. Do inquire about the hotel tax rate in the city where you intend to stay, when booking your accommodation.

Sales Tax

In the United States, the sales tax rate is set at state level, but in most states local counties can set an additional surtax. In some states, groceries and/or prescription drugs will be exempt from tax or charged at a lower rate. There are only five states that charge no state sales tax at all. They are Oregon, Delaware, New Hampshire, Alaska and Montana. Alaska allows a local tax rate not exceeding 7 percent and in Montana, local authorities are enabled to set a surtax rate, should they wish to do so. The state sales tax is generally set at between 4 percent (Alabama, Georgia, Louisiana, and Wyoming) and 7 percent (Indiana, Mississippi, New Jersey, Tennessee, Rhode Island) although there are exceptions outside that spectrum with Colorado at 2.8 percent and California at 7.5 percent. The local surcharge can be anything from 4.7 percent (Hawaii) to around 11 percent (Oklahoma and Louisiana). Can you claim back tax on your US purchases as a tourist? In the United States, sales tax is added retroactively upon payment, which means that it will not be included in the marked price of the goods you buy. Because it is set at state, rather than federal level, it is usually not refundable.

Two states do offer sales tax refunds to tourists. In Texas you will be able to get tax back from over 6000 participating stores if the tax amount came to more than $12 and the goods were purchased within 30 days of your departure. To qualify, you need to submit the original sales receipts, your passport, flight or transport information and visa details. Refunds are made in cash, cheque or via PayPal. Louisiana was the first state to introduce tax refunds for tourists. To qualify there, you must submit all sales receipts, together with your passport and flight ticket at a Refund Center outlet.

Tipping

Tipping is very common in the United States. In sit-down restaurants, a tip of between 10 and 15 percent of the bill is customary. At many restaurants, the salaries of waiting staff will be well below minimum wage levels. With large groups of diners, the restaurant may charge a mandatory gratuity, which is automatically included in the bill. At the trendiest New

York restaurants, a tip of 25 percent may be expected. While you can add a credit card tip, the best way to ensure the gratuity reaches your server is to tip separately in cash. Although tipping is less of an obligation at takeaway restaurants, such as McDonalds, you can leave your change, or otherwise $1, if there is a tip jar on the counter. In the case of pizza delivery, a minimum of $3 is recommended and more is obviously appreciated. Although a delivery charge is often levied, this money usually goes to the pizzeria, rather than the driver. Tip a taxi driver 10 percent of the total fare. At your hotel, tip the porter between $1 and $2 per bag. Tip between 10 and 20 percent at hair salons, spas, beauty salons and barber shops. Tip tour guides between 10 and 20 percent for a short excursion. For a day trip, tip both the guide and the driver $5 to $10 per person, if a gratuity is not included in the cost of the tour. Tip the drivers of charter or sightseeing buses around $1 per person.

Connectivity

Mobile Phones

There are four major service providers for wireless connection in the United States. They are Verizon Wireless, T-Mobile US, AT&T Mobility and Sprint. Not all are compatible with European standards. While most countries in Europe, Asia, the Middle East and East Africa uses the GSM mobile network, only two US service providers, T-Mobile and AT&T Mobility aligns with this. Also bear in mind that GSM carriers in the United States operate using the 850 MHz/1900 MHz frequency bands, whereas the UK, all of Europe, Asia, Australia and Africa use 900/1800MHz. You should check with your phone's tech specifications to find out whether it supports these standards. The other services, Verizon Wireless and Sprint use the CDMA network standard and, while Verizon's LTE frequencies are somewhat compatible with those of T-Mobile and AT&T, Sprint uses a different bandwidth for its LTE coverage.

To use your own phone, you can purchase a T-Mobile 3-in-1 starter kit for $20. If your device is unlocked, GMS-capable and supports either Band II (1900 MHz) or Band IV (1700/2100 MHz), you will be able to access the T-Mobile network. You can also purchase an AT&T sim card through the Go Phone Pay-as-you-go plan for as little as $0.99. Refill cards are available from $25 and are valid for 90 days. If you want to widen your network options, you may want to explore the market for a throwaway or disposable phone. At Walmart, you can buy non-contracted phones for as little as $9.99, as well as pre-paid sim cards and data top-up packages.

Canadians travellers will find the switch to US networks technically effortless, but should watch out for roaming costs. Several American networks do offer special international rates for calls to Canada or Mexico.

Dialing Code

The international dialing code for the United States is +1.

Emergency Numbers

General Emergency: 911 (this number can be used free of charge from any public phone in the United States).
MasterCard: 1-800-307-7309
Visa: 1-800-847-2911

General Information

Public Holidays

1 January: New Year's Day
3rd Monday in January: Martin Luther King Day
3rd Monday in February: President's Day
Last Monday in May: Memorial Day
4 July: Independence Day
1st Monday in September: Labour Day
2nd Monday in October: Columbus Day
11 November: Veteran's Day
4th Thursday in November: Thanksgiving Day
4th Friday in November: Day after Thanksgiving
25 December: Christmas Day (if Christmas Day falls on a Sunday, the Monday thereafter is a public holiday.) In some states, 26 December is a public holiday as well.

There are several festivals that are not public holidays per se, but are culturally observed in the United States. They include:

14 February: Valentine's Day
17 March: St Patrick's Day
March/April (variable): Easter or Passover
Second Sunday in May: Mother's Day
3rd Sunday in June: Father's Day
31 October: Halloween

Time Zones

The United States has 6 different time zones. **Eastern Standard Time** is observed in the states of Maine, New York, New Hampshire, Delaware, Vermont, Maryland, Rhode Island, Massachusetts, Connecticut, Pennsylvania, Ohio, North Carolina, South Carolina, Georgia, Virginia, West Virginia, Michigan, most of Florida and Indiana as well as the eastern parts of Kentucky and Tennessee. Eastern Standard Time is calculated as Greenwich Meantime/Coordinated Universal Time (UTC) -5. **Central Standard Time** is observed in Iowa, Illinois, Missouri, Arkansas, Louisiana, Oklahoma, Kansas, Mississippi, Alabama, near all of Texas, the western half of Kentucky, the central and western part of Tennessee, sections of the north-western and south-western part of Indiana, most of North and South Dakota, the eastern and central part of Nebraska and the north-western strip of Florida, also known as the Florida Panhandle. Central Standard Time is calculated as Greenwich Meantime/Coordinated Universal Time (UTC) -6. **Mountain Standard Time** is observed in New Mexico, Colorado, Wyoming, Montana, Utah, Arizona, the southern and central section of Idaho, the western parts of Nebraska, South Dakota and North Dakota, a portion of eastern Oregon and the counties of El Paso and Hudspeth in Texas. Mountain Standard Time is calculated as Greenwich Meantime/Coordinated Universal Time (UTC) -7. **Pacific Standard Time** is used in California, Washington, Nevada, most of Oregon and the northern part of Idaho. Pacific Standard Time is calculated as Greenwich Meantime/Coordinated Universal Time (UTC) -8. **Alaska Standard Time** is used in Alaska and this can be calculated as Greenwich Meantime/Coordinated Universal Time (UTC) -9. Because of its distant location, Hawaii is in a time zone of its own. **Hawaii Standard Time** can be calculated as Greenwich Meantime/Coordinated Universal Time (UTC) -10.

Daylight Savings Time

Clocks are set forward one hour at 2.00am on the second Sunday of March and set back one hour at 2.00am on the first Sunday of November for Daylight Savings Time. The states of Hawaii and Arizona do not observe Daylight Savings Time. However, the Navajo Indian Reservation, which extends across three states (Arizona, Utah and New Mexico), does observe Daylight Savings Time throughout its lands, including that portion which falls within Arizona.

School Holidays

In the United States, the academic year begins in September, usually in the week just before or after Labour Day and ends in the early or middle part of June. There is a Winter Break that includes Christmas and New Year and a Spring Break in March or April that coincides with Easter. In some states, there is also a Winter Break in February. The summer break occurs in the 10 to 11 weeks between the ending of one academic year and the commencement of the next academic year. Holidays may vary according to state and certain weather conditions such as hurricanes or snowfall may also lead to temporary school closures in affected areas.

Trading Hours

Trading hours in the United States vary. Large superstores like Walmart trade round the clock at many of its outlets, or else between 7am and 10pm. Kmart is often open from 8am to 10pm, 7 days a week. Target generally opens at 8am and may close at 10 or 11pm, depending on the area. Many malls will open at 10am and close at 9pm. Expect restaurants to be open from about 11am to 10pm or 11pm, although the hours of eateries that serve alcohol and bars may be restricted by local legislation. Banking hours also vary, according to branch and area. Branches of the Bank of America will generally open at 9am, and closing time can be anywhere between 4pm and 6pm. Most post office outlets are open from 9am to 5pm on weekdays.

Driving

In the United States, motorists drive on the right hand side of the road. As public transport options are not always adequate, having access to a car is virtually essential, when visiting the United States. To drive, you will need a valid driver's licence from your own country, in addition to an international driving permit. If your driver's licence does not include a photograph, you will be asked to submit your passport for identification as well.

For car rental, you will also need a credit card. Some companies do not rent out vehicles to drivers under the age of 25. Visitors with a UK license may need to obtain a check code for rental companies, should they wish to verify the details and validity of their driver's licence, via the DVLA view-your-licence service. This can also be generated online, but must be done at least 72 hours prior to renting the car. In most cases, though, the photo card type license will be enough. The largest rental companies - Alamo, Avis, Budget, Hertz, Dollar and Thrifty - are well represented in most major cities and usually have offices at international airports. Do check about the extent of cover included in your travel insurance package and credit card agreement. Some credit card companies may include Collision Damage Waiver (CDW), which will cover you against being held accountable for any damage to the rental car, but it is recommended that you also arrange for personal accident insurance, out-of-state insurance and supplementary liability insurance. You can sometimes cut costs on car rentals by reserving a car via the internet before leaving home.

The maximum speed limit in the United States varies according to state, but is usually between 100km per hour (65 m.p.h.) and 120km per hour (75 m.p.h.). For most of the Eastern states, as well as California and Oregon on the west coast the maximum speed driven on interstate highways should be 110km per hour (70 m.p.h.). Urban speed legislation varies, but in business and residential areas, speeds are usually set between 32km (20 miles) and 48km (30 miles) per hour. In Colorado, nighttime speed limits apply in certain areas where migrating wildlife could be endangered and on narrow, winding mountain passes, a limit of 32km (20 miles) per hour sometimes applies. In most American states there is a ban on texting for all drivers and a ban on all cell phone use for novice drivers.

Drinking

It is illegal in all 50 states for persons under the age of 21 to purchase alcohol or to be intoxicated. In certain states, such as Texas, persons between the age of 18 and 21 may be allowed to drink beer or wine, if in the company of a parent or legal guardian. In most states, the trading hours for establishments selling alcohol is limited. There are a few exceptions to this. In Nevada, alcohol may be sold round the clock and with few restrictions other than age. In Louisiana, there are no restrictions on trading in alcohol at state level, although some counties set their own restrictions. By contrast, Arizona has some of the strictest laws in relation to alcohol sales, consumption and driving under the influence. The sale of alcohol is prohibited on Native American reservations, unless the tribal council of that reservation has passed a vote to lift restrictions.

Smoking

There is no smoking ban set at federal level in the United States. At state level, there are 40 states in total that enact some form of state wide restriction on smoking, although the exemptions of individual states may vary. In Arizona, California, Colorado, Connecticut, Delaware, Hawaii, Illinois, Iowa, Kansas, Maine, Maryland, Massachusetts, Michigan, Minnesota, Montana, Nebraska, North Dakota, New Jersey, New Mexico, New York, Ohio, Oregon, Rhode Island, South Dakota, Utah, Vermont, Washington and Wisconsin, smoking is prohibited in all public enclosed areas, including bars and restaurants. The states of Arkansas, Florida, Indiana, Louisiana, Pennsylvania and Tennessee do have a general state wide restriction on smoking in public places, but exempt adult venues where under 21s are not allowed. This includes bars, restaurants, betting shops and gaming parlours (Indiana) and casinos (Louisiana and Pennsylvania). Nevada also has a state wide ban on smoking that exempts casinos, bars, strip clubs and brothels. In Georgia, state wide smoking legislation exempts bars and restaurants that only serve patrons over the age of 18. Idaho has a state wide ban that includes restaurants, but exempts bars serving only alcohol. New Hampshire, North Carolina and Virginia have also introduced some form of state wide smoking restriction. While the states of Alabama, Alaska, Kentucky, Mississippi, Missouri, Oklahoma, South Carolina, Texas, West Virginia and Wyoming have no state legislation, there are more specific restrictions at city and county level. In Arizona, there is an exemption for businesses located on Native American reservation and, in particular, for Native American religious ceremonies that may include smoking rituals. In California, the first state to implement anti-smoking legislation, smoking is also prohibited in parks and on sidewalks.

Electricity

Electricity: 110 volts
Frequency: 60 Hz

Electricity sockets are compatible with American Type A and Type B plugs. The Type A plug features two flat prongs or blades, while the Type B plug has the same plus an additional 'earth' prong. Most newer models of camcorders and cameras are dual voltage, which means that you should be able to charge them without an adapter in the United States, as they have a built in converter for voltage. You may find that appliances from the UK or Europe which were designed to accommodate a higher voltage will not function as effectively in the United States. While a current converter or transformer will be able to adjust the voltage, you may still experience some difficulty with the type of devices that are sensitive to variations in frequency as the United States uses 60 Hz, instead of the 50 Hz which is common in Europe and the UK. Appliances like hairdryers will usually be available in hotels and since electronic goods are fairly cheap in the United States, the easiest strategy may be to simply purchase a replacement. Bear in mind, that you may need an adaptor or transformer to operate it once you return home.

Food & Drink

Hamburgers, hot dogs and apple pie may be food items that come to mind when considering US culinary stereotypes, but Americans eat a wide variety of foods. They love steaks and ribs when dining out and pancakes or waffles for breakfast. As a society which embraces various immigrant communities, America excels at adopting and adapting traditional staples and adding its own touch to them. Several Asian favorites really originated in the United States. These include the California roll (offered in sushi restaurants) and the fortune cookie (chinese). Popular Hispanic imports include tacos, enchiladas and burritos. Another stereotype of American cuisine is large portion sizes. Hence the existence of American inventions such as the footlong sub, the footlong chilli cheese hot dog and the Krispy Creme burger, which combines a regular hamburger with a donut. Corn dogs are fairground favorites. Most menus are more balanced however. It is common to ask for a doggy bag (to take away remaining food) in a restaurant.

When in the South, enjoy corn bread, grits and southern fried chicken. Try spicy buffalo wings in New York, traditionally prepared baked beans in Boston and deep dish pizza in Chicago. French fries are favorites with kids of all ages, but Americans also love their potatoes as hash browns or the bite sized tater tots. Indulge your sweet tooth with Twinkies, pop tarts, cup cakes and banana splits. Popular sandwiches include the BLT (bacon, lettuce, tomato, the Reuben sandwich, the sloppy joe and the peanut butter and jelly.

Sodas (fizzy drinks) and bottled waters are the top beverages in the United States. The top selling soft drinks are Coca Cola, followed by Pepsi Cola, Diet Coke, Mountain Dew and Dr Pepper. In America's colonial past, tea was initially the hot beverage of choice and it was tea politics that kicked off the American Revolution, but gradually tea has been replaced by coffee in popularity. From the 1970s, Starbucks popularized coffee culture in the United States. Americans still drink gallons of tea and they are particularly fond of a refreshing glass of iced tea. Generally, Americans drink more beer than wine and favorite brands include Bud Light, followed by Coors Light, Budweiser and Miller Light. Popular cocktails are the Martini, the Manhattan, the Margarita, the Bloody Mary, the Long Island Ice tea and Sex on the Beach.

American Sports

Baseball is widely regarded as the national sport of America. The sport originated in the mid 1800s and superficially shares the basic objective of cricket, which is to score runs by hitting a ball pitched by the opposing team, but in baseball, the innings ends as soon as three players have been caught out. A point is scored when a runner has passed three bases and reached the 4th or home base of the baseball diamond. After 9 innings, the team with the highest number of runs is declared the winner. The Baseball World Series is played in the fall (autumn), usually in October, and consists of best-of-seven play-off between the two top teams representing the rival affiliations of the National League and American League.

Although the origins of American football can be found in rugby, the sport is now widely differentiated from its roots and today numerous distinctions exist between the two. In American football, a game is divided into four quarters, with each team fielding 11 players, although unlimited substitution is allowed. Players wear helmets and heavy padding as any player can be tackled, regardless of ball possession. An annual highlight is the Super Bowl, the championship game of the National Football League. The event is televised live to over a 100 million viewers and features a high profile halftime performance by a top music act. Super bowl Sunday traditionally takes place on the first Sunday of February.

The roots of stock car racing can be found in America's prohibition era, when bootleggers needed powerful muscle cars (often with modifications for greater speed) to transport their illicit alcohol stocks. Informal racing evolved to a lively racing scene in Daytona, Florida. An official body, NASCAR, was founded in 1948 to regulate the sport, NASCAR. Today, NASCAR racing has millions of fans. One of its most prestigious events is the Sprint Cup, a championship which comprises of 36 races and kicks off each year with the Daytona 500.

Rodeo originated from the chores and day-to-day activities of Spanish cattle farmers and later, the American ranchers who occupied the former Spanish states such as Texas, California and Arizona. The advent of fencing eliminated the need for cattle drives, but former cowboys found that their skills still offered good entertainment, providing a basis for wild west shows such as those presented by Buffalo Bill. Soon, rodeo events became the highlight of frontier towns throughout the west. During the first half of the 20th centuries, organizations formed to regulate events. Today, rodeo is considered a legitimate national sport with millions of fans. If you want to experience the thrill of this extreme sport, attend one of its top events. The Prescott Frontier Days show in Arizona is billed to be America's oldest rodeo. The Reno Rodeo in Nevada is a 10 day event that takes place in mid-June and includes the option of closer participation as a volunteer. Rodeo Houston, a large 20 day event that takes place towards the end of winter, is coupled to a livestock show. Visit the San Antonio show in Texas during February for the sheer variety of events. The National Western Rodeo in Denver Colorado is an indoor event that attracts up to half a million spectators each year. The National Finals that takes place in Las Vegas during December is the prestigious championship that marks the end of the year's rodeo calendar.

Useful Websites

https://esta.cbp.dhs.gov/esta/ -- The US Electronic System for Travel Authorization
http://www.visittheusa.com/
http://roadtripusa.com/
http://www.roadtripamerica.com/
http://www.road-trip-usa.info/
http://www.autotoursusa.com/
http://www.onlyinyourstate.com/
http://www.theamericanroadtripcompany.co.uk/